W9-BMP-664

SPACE MYTHS, BUSTED!

by Angie Smibert

12 STORY LIBRARY

www.12StoryLibrary.com

12-Story Library is an imprint of Peterson Publishing Company and Press Room Editions.

Produced for 12-Story Library by Red Line Editorial

Photographs ©: NASA, cover, 1, 8, 11, 18, 19, 28; NASA/CXC/UMass Amherst/Q.D.Wang et al, 4; Tony Hallas, 5; James McArdell/Library of Congress, 6; NASA/ESA, 7; Comstock/Stockbyte/Thinkstock, 9; NASA/JPL, 10, 12; Orren Jack Turner/Library of Congress, 13; Bettmann/Corbis, 14; NASA/AIA, 15, 29; NASA/CXC/MPE/J/SDSS, 16; NASA/ESA/D. Coe/N. Benitez/T. Broadhurst/H. Ford, 17; NASA/JPL-Caltech/Space Science Institute, 20; NASA/JPL/Space Science Institute, 21; NASA/JHUAPL/SwRI, 22; NASA, ESA, and A. Schaller (for STScI), 23; NASA Ames/W Stenzel; SETI Institute/D Caldwell, 24; NASA, ESA, and G. Bacon (STScI), 25; NASA/JPL-Caltech/GSFC/JAXA, 26; NASA Ames/JPL-Caltech/T. Pyle, 27

Library of Congress Cataloging-in-Publication Data
Names: Smibert, Angie, author.
Title: Space myths, busted! / by Angie Smibert.
Description: North Mankato, MN : 12-Story Library, [2017] | Series: Science
    myths, busted! | Audience: Grades 4 to 6. | Includes bibliographical
    references and index.
Identifiers: LCCN 2016002366| ISBN 9781632353054 (library bound : alk. paper)
    | ISBN 9781632353559 (pbk. : alk. paper)
Subjects: LCSH: Astronomy--Miscellanea--Juvenile literature. | Errors,
    Scientific--Juvenile literature. | Outer space--Miscellanea--Juvenile
    literature. | Outer space--Exploration--Miscellanea--Juvenile literature.
Classification: LCC QB46 .S6125 2017 | DDC 520--dc23
LC record available at http://lccn.loc.gov/2016002366

Printed in the United States of America
Mankato, MN
May, 2016

Table of Contents

Busted: The Milky Way Is All There Is

In the early 1900s, no one knew how vast the universe really was. But that changed in 1920. That year, American astronomer Harlow Shapley accurately measured Earth's galaxy, the Milky Way. According to his calculations, it was 100,000 light-years across. He and many other astronomers argued that was it. The Milky Way *was* the universe. Other astronomers disagreed. Heber Curtis thought Earth's galaxy was one of many. But he and his

Scientists continue to study the Milky Way.

supporters had no proof of that. Then, Edwin Hubble made the first of two key discoveries that busted Shapley's hypothesis.

In 1919, Hubble worked at the Mt. Wilson Observatory in California. The observatory's 100-inch Hooker Telescope was the biggest telescope of its day. With it, Hubble took thousands of photographs of spiral nebulae over time. On October 4, 1924, he was comparing photos of the Andromeda Nebula. He discovered a Cepheid variable. A Cepheid is the one kind of star astronomers use to accurately measure distance. Shapley had used a Cepheid to make his calculations in 1920. Using the Cepheid in Andromeda, Hubble discovered it was 900,000 light-years away. Andromeda was outside our galaxy— way outside of it.

Later, astronomers found Hubble's new number was incorrect.

The
Andromeda
Galaxy

Andromeda was actually more than twice that distance from Earth. But Hubble's discovery still busted Shapley's theory. Hubble also discovered Andromeda itself was a galaxy. The Milky Way was not the only galaxy in the universe. Now, fewer than 100 years later, scientists know there are at least 100 billion galaxies out there. That number is likely to increase, too. New technologies and research methods may reveal even more galaxies.

2.54 million

Distance, in light-years, from Earth to the Andromeda galaxy.

THE SHAPLEY-CURTIS DEBATE

On April 26, 1920, astronomers Harlow Shapley and Heber Curtis held a debate in Washington, DC. They argued about the size of the universe. Shapley argued the universe ended at the limits of Earth's galaxy. Curtis argued the Milky Way was one of many "island universes." Astronomers now call this the Great Debate.

- In 1920, Shapley measured the Milky Way to be 100,000 light-years wide.
- Four years later, Hubble found a star in Andromeda that was nine times farther away than Shapley thought.
- This proved Andromeda was outside Earth's galaxy, and the universe was much bigger than previously thought.

Busted: Space Is Standing Still

In 1687, Sir Isaac Newton published the first volume of his famous work, *Principia Mathematica*. In it, he outlined his laws of gravity and motion. He also described his belief that the universe is infinite and unmoving. For hundreds of years, scientists firmly believed Newton's vision of the universe. In the twentieth century, Albert Einstein calculated that the universe was expanding. But he thought he must have made a mistake. He came up with a mathematical explanation that would account for the movement.

Sir Isaac Newton thought the universe was stationary.

70

Estimated kilometers per second per megaparsec at which the universe is expanding.

- Until the early twentieth century, most scientists thought the universe was stationary.
- Hubble discovered galaxies were actually moving away from Earth and everything else in the universe.
- This meant the universe is expanding.

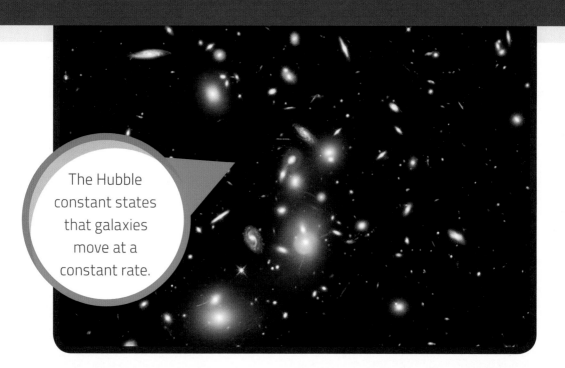

The Hubble constant states that galaxies move at a constant rate.

He later called this his greatest blunder.

In 1929, Edwin Hubble made another astonishing discovery. After discovering Andromeda, he and his assistant, Milton Humason, identified and catalogued galaxies. They also measured each galaxy's Doppler shift. That is the change in the length of light or sound waves. The waves change length as the observer and galaxy move apart or toward each other. Hubble and Humason found all galaxies are moving away from Earth—and away from each other. They did so at a consistent rate now called the Hubble constant. The universe was not standing still. As Einstein's calculations had predicted, it was actually expanding. This discovery rocked the scientific community.

THE BIG BANG THEORY

If the universe is expanding, where did it start? Scientists reasoned it must have begun in one place and at one moment in the past. In 1949, George Gamow proposed a theory that would explain the origin of the universe. He called it the Big Bang Theory. The universe started in an explosion from a single, tiny point and expanded outward. It is still going.

Busted: The Universe Is 6,000 Years Old

In the seventeenth century, scientists such as Isaac Newton and Johannes Kepler theorized about when the universe was created. They used various methods, including astronomy and historical research, to make their calculations. Newton's calculations led him to believe the universe was created in 3998 BCE. Kepler believed it was created in 3993 BCE.

Soon, much of the Western world believed the universe was a mere 6,000 years old. These hypotheses stood for the next two and a half centuries.

But scientists continued to study the age of the universe. By the mid-nineteenth century, they had become skeptical Earth was 6,000 years old. Numerous scientific discoveries, particularly in geology, told scientists that Earth was much, much older. Scientists estimated the earth was between 20 million and several billion years old. In 1905, radiometric dating confirmed Earth was 4.5 billion years old. But what about the universe?

Modern astronomers can calculate the age of the

Early scientists thought the universe, including Earth, was just 6,000 years old.

Scientists study Earth's rocks and soil to determine its age.

universe in several ways. One uses the Hubble constant. The constant tells astronomers how fast the universe is moving. Astronomers use this number to calculate how long ago the Big Bang happened. The universe is between 10 and 20 billion years old.

13 billion

Current average estimate, in years, for the age of the universe.

- Scientists such as Newton and Kepler calculated the age of the universe to be 6,000 years old.
- In the twentieth century, scientists discovered the earth was millions of years old.
- Using the Hubble constant, scientists now believe the universe to be 10 to 20 billion years old.

THINK ABOUT IT

It took scientists hundreds of years to discover the true age of the universe. Now scientists believe they have the answer. Do you think it is possible for that number to change in the future? What discoveries could make scientists change their theories?

Busted: Our Solar System Has Only Six Planets

Humans have known about the first six planets in Earth's solar system for thousands of years. Mercury, Venus, Mars, Saturn, and Jupiter are visible to the naked eye. In March 1781, astronomer William Herschel added a seventh. He spotted a tiny, fuzzy object he thought was a comet. He then noticed it had a circular orbit. It was a planet, not a comet. Herschel called the planet Uranus. It was the first new planet discovered in recorded history.

Decades after its discovery, astronomers noticed something odd about Uranus. It made its journey around the sun slightly faster than predicted. Some astronomers guessed another planet beyond Uranus was making Uranus's orbit faster. Mathematicians John Couch Adams and Urbain Le Verrier used Newton's laws of gravity to find the other planet. They independently calculated a prediction of where it might be. Then, German astronomer Johann Galle used these calculations to search for Neptune in the night sky. Galle was the first to observe the planet Neptune on September 9, 1896.

Uranus was the first planet discovered that could not be seen with the naked eye.

More than 100 years after finding Uranus, scientists discovered Neptune.

NEWTON'S LAW OF UNIVERSAL GRAVITATION

In 1727, Newton described gravity as the force keeping moons and planets in their orbits. The gravitational force between two bodies depends on their size and the distance between them. Bigger objects have more pull than smaller ones. For instance, a star has more pull than a planet. Planets close together pull on each other more than those farther apart.

84

Number of Earth-years Uranus takes to orbit the Sun.

- Humans have known about the first six planets since before recorded history.
- Herschel discovered Uranus in 1781.
- Mathematicians used Newton's laws of gravity to locate another new planet, Neptune.

Busted:
Planet Vulcan Exists

Nineteenth-century astronomers observed Mercury's orbit was odd. It was not acting according to Newton's laws of gravity. Today, scientists know Mercury has an elliptical orbit. But in the nineteenth century, astronomers believed another planet was to blame. They thought this mystery planet was between Mercury and the Sun. It was pulling Mercury into this odd orbit. They asked Le Verrier to calculate the position of the missing planet. He had already done so for Uranus.

Based on his calculations, Le Verrier thought the planet should be easily visible. He called it Vulcan after the Roman god of fire. He asked astronomers to pay special attention to sun spots. One of these might be the shadow of Vulcan crossing the path of the Sun. In December 1859, Le Verrier received a letter from an amateur astronomer. He claimed to have seen a circular object passing across the sun on March 26, 1859. Le Verrier believed it was Vulcan. Other astronomers, however, could not confirm his findings. Le Verrier calculated the object was too small to affect Mercury.

The search continued. For the next decade, astronomers began to doubt the existence of Vulcan. Those doubts persisted into the twentieth century. Astronomers could

Mercury's odd orbit convinced scientists another planet existed between it and the sun.

9th

Planet in the solar system Vulcan would have been if it existed.

- Nineteenth-century astronomers observed Mercury's odd orbit and believed it was caused by another unknown planet.
- They searched for Vulcan for decades.
- In the twentieth century, Einstein's new theory about gravity solved the Mercury mystery.

EINSTEIN'S GRAVITY

Newton believed gravity pulled on an object like a rubber band does. Einstein believed gravity warped the fabric of space and time. Imagine a piece of fabric pulled tight. That is space. When a heavy object—such as a planet—sits on it, the fabric stretches and dips according to how massive the object is. That dip is gravity.

not find Vulcan. Yet nothing quite explained Mercury's odd orbit—until 1915. That year, Albert Einstein resolved the problem of Mercury's orbit using his new theories on gravity. He believed gravity changed relative to the distance between two bodies in motion. Changes in the pull of gravity would change a body's orbit. Changing gravity explained Mercury's odd orbit. This theory radically altered our view on how gravity really works.

Einstein's theories about gravity helped explain Mercury's orbit.

Busted: Stars Are Made of Iron

In 1859, scientists Gustav Kirchoff and Robert Bunsen heated up various chemical elements. They looked at the range of wavelengths of light the elements gave off. Each element emitted a distinct set of lines within the light. The pattern was like a fingerprint to identify elements. A few years later, astronomers William and Margaret Huggins made a related discovery. The light from stars contained the same lines as Earth's elements. They concluded stars were made up of the same elements as planets. Most planets have heavy elements, such as iron, at their cores. This led some astronomers to believe stars must be superheated, heavy planets.

But in 1925, astronomer Cecilia Payne set the record straight. She discovered the sun and other stars were nearly entirely made up of hydrogen and helium. These are the two lightest elements. Heavier elements make up only 2 percent

Payne discovered the sun was made of gas, not iron.

of the mass of stars. But many of her fellow astronomers doubted her findings. How could hydrogen and helium fuel a star?

The answer became clear in the 1930s. Scientists made key discoveries in nuclear physics. In 1938, Charles Critchfield and Hans Bethe theorized the core of the sun ran on nuclear fusion. The sun fuses hydrogen atoms together to form helium. This releases enormous energy that powers the sun.

The sun is a very hot and unsettled body of gas.

75
Percent of the mass of the universe made up of hydrogen.

- Before the 1920s, astronomers thought stars were superheated planets.
- Payne discovered stars are primarily made up of the lightest two elements: hydrogen and helium.
- Stars fuse hydrogen together to make helium, releasing enormous energy.

OUR SUN

Just like other stars, the sun is made of plasma. Plasma is an extremely hot and electrically charged gas. Temperatures at the core can reach 15.7 million degrees Kelvin (28 million° F). That is where fusion happens. The surface of the sun is only 5,800 degrees Kelvin (10,000° F).

Busted: Everything in the Universe Is Visible

In 1933, Swiss astronomer Fritz Zwicky was studying the Coma Cluster. He was measuring how fast the galaxies in the cluster were moving. He noticed something odd. The visible part of the cluster was moving too fast for its small size. He calculated that the cluster had to be 400 times larger than it looked. Much of the cluster was not visible. Zwicky concluded that something must be holding the Coma Cluster together. He called it dark matter.

The huge Coma cluster is at least 500,000 light-years across.

Dark matter is material that humans or telescopes cannot see. Scientists do not yet know precisely what makes up dark matter. It may consist of dust or intergalactic gas. Dark matter may contain planets, burned-out stars, and black holes. It may be a type of undiscovered particle. Or, dark matter may be a combination of all of these.

For years, other scientists did not accept Zwicky's idea of dark matter. Then, other astronomers began to

DARK ENERGY

In 1998, scientists discovered the universe was expanding fast. It was growing more quickly than it did a very long time ago. This was a shocking discovery. Scientists thought the expansion of the universe was *slowing* because of gravity. Somewhere, the universe contained more energy than suspected or is measurable. Scientists call this dark energy. Approximately 68 percent of the universe may be made of dark energy.

make similar observations. Vera Rubin was a student of physicist George Gamow. She noticed stars at the edge of the galaxy rotate much faster than expected. Given the galaxy's mass, the stars should have moved more slowly. She concluded that galaxies are much larger than what humans can see. This is true even through the most powerful telescope. Perhaps as much as 27 percent of each galaxy is made up of dark matter.

4

Percent of the universe that astronomers have been able to detect.

- Swiss astronomer Zwicky discovered dark matter.
- Dark matter is material that humans and human technology cannot detect.
- It may contain dust, gas, planets, stars, black holes, or even undiscovered particles.

The Hubble Space Telescope's images allowed astronomers to infer where dark matter was in galaxy cluster Abell 1689.

Busted: The Moon Was Once Part of Earth

For centuries, the moon's origin puzzled scientists. People have had many theories about the moon's beginning. In 1898, astronomer George Darwin had an idea. He theorized that the moon had split off from the earth. He believed it did so when the planet was still being formed. Some scientists thought Earth had captured the Moon in its orbit. Other astronomers

THINK ABOUT IT

How did Apollo 11 help us understand the Moon's origins? Find evidence in the text to support your answer.

thought the earth and moon had formed at the same time.

In 1969, the astronauts of Apollo 11 walked on the moon. They took

Buzz Aldrin walks on the moon in 1969 as part of the Apollo 11 mission.

samples from the moon's surface. Scientists examined the moon rocks and lunar soil. They realized none of the moon theories was right. Instead, scientists proposed a new theory based on their new evidence. It is called the Giant Impact Theory. It says more than 4 billion years ago, an object the size of Mars glanced off Earth. This occurred shortly after Earth was formed. Rocky debris from both the earth and the object spewed out into orbit. Over time, this debris formed the moon.

The moon rocks and lunar soil scientists collected contained elements found only on Earth. This meant at least part of the moon came from Earth. But the moon had far less iron than Earth. It could not have simply been part of the earth at some point. A collision with Earth could explain how Earth's elements showed up in the lunar samples.

4.5 billion
Number of years ago the moon started to form.

- Before the 1970s, astronomers had three main theories about how the moon was formed.
- Evidence from the Apollo missions supports the Giant Impact Theory.
- Scientists learned that part of the moon came from the earth after a planet-sized object hit Earth.

Scientists believe the moon was created after an object collided with Earth.

Busted: Saturn Is the Only Planet with Rings

In 1610, Galileo observed that Saturn had rings. He spied them through the telescope he had just invented. For the next 367 years, scientists thought only Saturn had rings. Then in 1977, astronomers were studying Uranus's atmosphere. They observed the planet as it passed in front of a distant red star. They noticed a flicker right before Uranus blocked out the star's light. There was something very thin and

> For nearly four centuries, scientists believed only Saturn had rings.

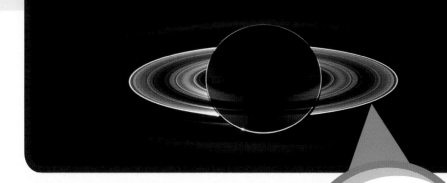

This 2006 image shows the many smaller rings that orbit Saturn.

close to the planet. Uranus had rings. At the time, observers counted nine rings. In 1986, the Voyager 2 spacecraft's cameras recorded two more rings. The Hubble Space Telescope brought the count up to 13 in 2003.

Now, astronomers know all of the giant planets in the solar system have rings. So do a few moons. In 1979, Voyager 2 spotted rings around Jupiter. In 1989, it recorded Neptune's rings. But not all ring systems look like Saturn's. Jupiter's are narrower and darker. Neptune's are thin and lumpy.

6

Number of rings around Neptune.

- Galileo discovered Saturn's rings in 1610.
- In 1977, scientists observed rings around Uranus.
- Voyager 2 also found rings around Jupiter and Neptune.

WHAT IS IN A RING?

From Earth, Saturn's rings look like solid bands. But the rings are actually made of orbiting bodies. These moons, asteroids, and meteoroids are made of ice and rock. They orbit Saturn very quickly. The rings look solid from a distance. It looks like Saturn has only seven rings. But each of these large rings is really many small rings.

Busted:
Pluto Is a Planet

Nineteenth-century astronomer Percival Lowell was convinced a planet lay beyond Neptune. He called it Planet X. Lowell spent years searching for it. He even founded an observatory in Arizona to carry on this work. But he died in 1916 before finding Planet X. In 1929, amateur astronomer Clyde Tombaugh arrived at the Lowell Observatory. He photographed the sky in search of the mysterious planet. After combing through pictures for many months, he finally spotted it. On March 3, 1930, Lowell's birthday, Tombaugh announced he had found the ninth planet. He called it Pluto.

For 76 years, Pluto was considered a planet. But then astronomers began to have doubts. In August 1992, astronomers at the University of Hawaii made a discovery.

Pluto (foreground) is now considered a dwarf planet.

Astronomers began to rethink what makes a planet a planet. In 2006, the International Astronomical Union (IAU) clarified what defines a planet. A planet orbits the sun. In doing so, it clears its path of other objects. A planet is massive enough to be basically round. Pluto was round and orbited the sun. But it was surrounded by other objects. Its path was not clear. Under the new definition, Pluto was not a planet. So the IAU adopted a new classification: dwarf planet.

In 2005, scientists discovered Eris, another dwarf planet, near Pluto.

They observed the first of many thousands of objects orbiting beyond Neptune. Pluto seemed to be only one of these objects. They all roughly shared Pluto's orbit around the sun. In 2003, astronomers found an object bigger than Pluto. It even had a moon.

5
Number of dwarf planets discovered in the solar system as of fall 2015.

- Many astronomers thought there could be another planet beyond Neptune's orbit.
- In 1930, Tombaugh finally found it and called it Pluto.
- In 2006, Pluto was reclassified as a dwarf planet after the IAU redefined what makes a planet a planet.

THINK ABOUT IT

Not everyone was happy when scientists reclassified Pluto. Do you believe that calling Pluto a dwarf planet was the right decision? Why or why not? Use evidence from the text to support your answer.

Busted: The Outer Solar System Is Empty

Pluto was discovered in 1930. Most scientists thought its orbit marked the outer edge of the solar system. Mystery remained, however. No one had discovered where comets come from. In 1932, Estonian astronomer Ernst Opik theorized they started beyond the newly discovered planet. In 1950, Dutch astronomer Jan Oort observed the orbits of 19 comets. He came up with a similar idea. He thought comets with orbits lasting longer than 200 years came from a distant region. It is now called the Oort Cloud. At the same time, astronomers Gerard Kuiper and Kenneth Edgeworth were at work. Independently, they theorized a belt of comets with shorter orbits existed just beyond Neptune. This region became known as the Kuiper Belt. But for many decades, they could not prove it existed. No evidence supported the claim that our solar system contained anything beyond Neptune except Pluto.

But proof did come in 1992. Scientists found the first Kuiper Belt Object (KBO) that year. Since then, scientists have discovered more than 1,000 KBOs.

Scientists believe this comet is from a region far beyond the solar system.

Three dwarf planets are part of these discoveries. Scientists think the Kuiper Belt may contain more than 100,000 objects. No proof of the Oort Cloud has been found yet.

But some astronomers think a very distant KBO, Sedna, might be part it. Sedna has an elliptical orbit. Its orbit is 1,000 astronomical units from the sun. That is more than 1,000 times the distance from the earth to the sun.

30
Astronomical units between the start of the Kuiper Belt and the sun.

- After Pluto was discovered, astronomers theorized a comet cloud existed in the outer solar system.
- Astronomers Kuiper and Edgeworth independently proposed another belt of comets in the early 1950s.
- Scientists now know of at least 1,000 objects in the Kuiper Belt.

OORT CLOUD

Astronomers think a cloud of comets orbits the sun. They believe the Oort Cloud is far beyond the outermost planets and the Kuiper Belt. Its outer edge is 100,000 times the distance between the sun and the earth. When passing other stars, the orbits of the Oort Cloud's comets may be disturbed. The comets could head either toward the other star or the sun.

25

Busted: Our Sun Is the Only Star with Planets

Astronomers have been looking for planets outside the solar system for more than a century. A few nineteenth-century astronomers thought they had spotted a planet in another star system. But they could not be sure. The technology to prove the existence of extrasolar or exoplanets was not invented yet. It would not be until the late twentieth century.

> The sun is not the only star with planets orbiting around it.

In 1991, radio astronomers discovered the first true exoplanet. Alexander Wolszczan and Dale Frail looked at the radio signals of the star PSRB1257. They noticed a variation in these signals. The variation meant something was orbiting the star. For the next few decades, astronomers discovered many other exoplanets. Some exoplanets even have atmospheres.

In 1999, astronomers observed the shadow of a planet passing across the star HD209458. In 2000, astronomers reviewed images from the Hubble Space Telescope. They observed this planet had an atmosphere. In 2004, the telescope

Astronomers continue to discover exoplanets, including Kepler-186f in 2015.

took pictures of the dust disc around another star. When astronomers analyzed the photos, they found a planet. This was the first exoplanet seen using visible light.

1,911
Number of extrasolar planets discovered as of November 2015.

- Astronomers have been searching for planets outside the solar system for more than a century.
- Astronomers detected the first exoplanet in 1991.
- The first photograph of an exoplanet was not taken until 2004.

Fact Sheet

- National Aeronautics and Space Administration (NASA) scientists have been exploring space since 1958. Since then, NASA has launched dozens of missions to explore Earth, the solar system, and the universe. The Apollo program landed the first human on the moon. Today, NASA spacecraft explore Mars, Pluto, and points beyond the solar system.

- Astronomers hope to find an exoplanet that could sustain life. They believe the exoplanet would be approximately Earth's size and orbit a star. It would need to be close enough to the star so liquid water was present. If it were too close, it would be too hot. If it were too far, frigid temperatures would make the exoplanet unlivable.

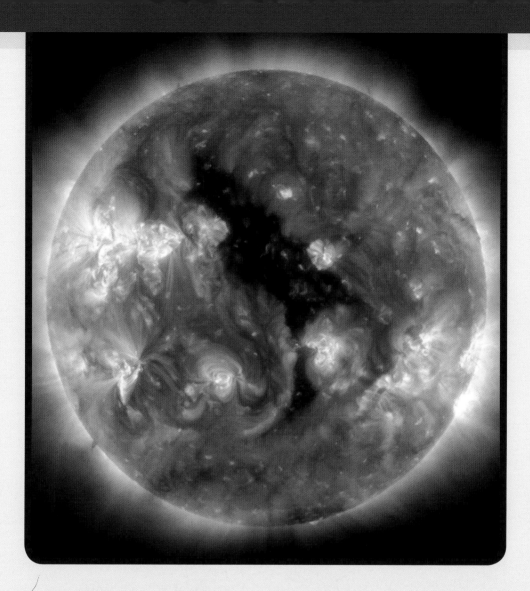

Astronauts from the United States, Russia, China, and 12 other countries have studied space aboard the International Space Station. They study space's effect on plant and animal biology and on human health. They test new technologies that could be used in future space exploration.

For decades, only national governments could afford to develop spacecraft and run a space program. But that has changed since the turn of the twenty-first century. Private companies are developing their own spacecraft. Space X and Virgin Galactic are only two examples.

Glossary

astronomical unit
A unit of distance equal to the distance between the earth and the sun, approximately 93 million miles (150 million km).

comet
An object in space with a center of ice and dust and a tail of gas and dust particles.

element
One of the basic substances made up of atoms.

elliptical
Oval.

galaxy
Any one of the very large group of stars that make up the universe.

gravity
A natural force that tends to cause physical things to move toward each other.

light-year
A unit of distance equal to the distance light travels in one year, approximately 5.88 trillion miles (9.46 trillion km).

megaparsec
A unit of distance equal to about 3.3 million light-years.

nebulae
Huge clouds of gas or dust in deep space.

nuclear
Related to the center, or nucleus, of an atom.

radiometric
Relating to the rate of the breakdown of elements that give off energy when their atoms are broken up.

For More Information

Books

Aguilar, David A. *Space Encyclopedia: A Tour of Our Solar System & Beyond.* Washington, DC: National Geographic, 2013.

Marlowe, Christie. *Space Telescopes.* Vestal, NY: Village Earth Press, 2014.

Taylor-Butler, Christine. *The Moon.* New York: Children's Press, 2014.

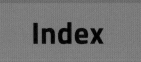

Index

About the Author

Angie Smibert is the author of several young adult science fiction novels. She was also a writer and online training developer at NASA's Kennedy Space Center for many years. She received NASA's prestigious Silver Snoopy and several other awards for her work.

READ MORE FROM 12-STORY LIBRARY

Every 12-Story Library book is available in many formats. For more information, visit 12StoryLibrary.com.